از حبت دردها درمان شود

Through Love Pain Is Healed

101 Poems of the Heart

by Rumi

OTHER WORKS BY RASOUL SHAMS
Published by the Rumi Poetry Club

Rumi: The Art of Loving

Rumi Essays: On the Life, Poetry, and Vision of the Greatest Persian Sufi Poet

The Words of Rumi: Celebrating a Year of Inspiration

This book belongs to

Jalâluddin Rumi

THROUGH LOVE PAIN IS HEALED

101 Poems of the Heart

*Selected and Translated by
Rasoul Shams*

RUMI PUBLICATIONS
an imprint of
RUMI POETRY CLUB
2023

Through Love Pain Is Healed
101 Poems of the Heart by Rumi

By Jalâluddin Rumi

Selected and translated by Rasoul Shams

Rumi Publications, an imprint of Rumi Poetry Club

Copyright © 2023 Rumi Poetry Club

All rights reserved.

No part of this book may be published, reproduced, translated or transmitted in any form or by any means without written permission of the publisher, except in the case of brief quotations (with citation) embodied in critical articles, dissertations or reviews.

ISBN-13: 978-0-9850568-7-2 (paperback)

ISBN-10: 0-9850568-7-8 (paperback)

ISBN-13: 978-0-9850568-8-9 (eBook)

ISBN-10: 0-9850568-8-6 (eBook)

Library of Congress Control Number: 2023941954

First Published in 2023

Rumi Poetry Club

P.O. Box 521376

Salt Lake City, UT 84152-1376

www.rumipoetryclub.com

Published in the United States of America

CONTENTS

Foreword... **13**

Longing..**15**

    1. Listen 17

    2. Through love..................................... 18

    3. Fire of love 19

    4. The heart is a candle........................20

    5. As you walk 21

    6. If you 22

    7. Someone asked 23

    8. Seeking union 24

    9. Seek thirst 25

    10. You, I desire 26

    11. Love says 28

    12. The sky is in love 29

    13. Branches 30

    14. Enter the fire 31

    15. Friends...32

Map of the heart......................................**33**

    16. Love stays awake 35

17. A stranger in this world 36
18. Finding a home 37
19. Where God resides 38
20. A pure mirror 39
21. Shining heart 40
22. Purifying water 41
23. Crystal clear 42
24. A window to light 43
25. So buoyant 44
26. Origin of the heart 45
27. Source of all songs 46
28. Dance until dawn 47
29. Face of the heart 48
30. Rays of light 49
31. Beneath the tongue 50
32. Lips shut tight 51
33. Path of the heart 52
34. Graceful ocean 53
35. Without you 54
36. Gate of Paradise 55
37. Even if 56
38. Green garden 57
39. Garden in the ocean 58
40. Chattering mouth 59
41. Will they understand? 60

Union **61**

    42. Created in pairs 63

    43. Red wine 64

    44. They say 65

    45. Like the wave 66

    46. A hundred days 67

    47. Fusion 68

    48. Soul of the world 70

    49. Fragrance of love 72

    50. Be with me 73

    51. Inside the eye 74

    52. Only one light 75

    53. How I became human 76

    54. You and I 78

Agony **79**

    55. Ups and downs 81

    56. I asked love 82

    57. Love-madness 83

    58. Inside the ruined heart 84

    59. Dark shadow 85

    60. Healing medicine 86

    61. Sorrows of the world 87

    62. The real step 88

    63. Fear not 89

    64. Agony of love 90

    65. Now run 91

66. I am ripe 92

67. I have chosen you..................................93

68. Love is a mystery 94

Ecstasy 95

69. This love 97

70. Delight.. 98

71. Never, never...99

72. I will win life..100

73. I became alive..................................... 101

74. All particles are lovers 102

75. Only one step.......................................103

76. Die in this love 104

77. As long as I live...................................105

78. Most wondrous 106

79. Wind and leaf 107

80. Shining like the sun............................108

81. Consider this 109

82. Love is this 110

Living 111

83. Plant seeds of love 113

84. Source of all joy 114

85. Water of life 115

86. History of lovers 116

87. Days of life...117

88. Love is for the living........................... 118

89. The unseen.. 119

90. The book 120
91. Empty bowl 121
92. Stay by her side... 122
93. Diamond-sharp sword 123
94. Who am I?.. 124
95. A divine person 126
96. Our sweet words 128
97. Fear of death 129
98. Religion of love 130
99. Neither captive nor captor 131
100. Arrived 132
101. Outcome of my life 133

Sources **135**
Acknowledgments **138**

FOREWORD

For nearly four decades I have enjoyed reading the works of Jalaluddin Rumi, the thirteenth-century Persian poet and mystic. The single key word – the common thread – that runs through the entirety of Rumi's poems is love. Rumi is a prominent teacher in the school of love; his spiritual path is the path of love. This book is a collection of Rumi's best-known poems on various facets of love. It is perhaps interesting to find out what an eight-hundred-year-old poet has to say about love and the inner workings of the heart. Rumi's words and vision are very relevant to our times; they have survived through centuries because of their elegance and profoundness. His wisdom of love is perennial.

We sometimes divide love into divine and human, heavenly and earthly, sacred and secular, spiritual and physical. For Rumi, however, as the poems in this book reveal, all kinds of love – that is genuine heart-felt, non-selfish love – comes from one and the same source. We may express our love to God, nature, family, friends, goodness, beauty or truth; but loving is rooted in the heart where also God, intimacy, courage, sincerity, and serenity reside.

This is a book of poetry – not of the pen but of the heart. There are no philosophical arguments here, nor are there any negative judgments passed on other experiences and expressions. Rumi simply shares his own findings. Read these poems as they speak to your heart and as they soothe your soul. Rumi's constituency is the human heart, and its field stretches the expanse of compassion, passion, pain, union, ecstasy, and presence.

This is a book of the poetry of love. Love is therapeutic; love is all-inclusive. Through love everyone is healed. Love does not solve our problems in the manner of satisfying our ego or greed. In the alchemy of love, problems are dissolved. Spiritual poetry essentially wants to open our hearts to a deep consciousness and compassion. True love arises from a deep sense of oneness.

The selection, arrangement, and translation of the poems in this anthology are mine. But the original work and words belong to the great poet and master of the heart - Rumi. The book title comes from the second poem in this volume. Titles for the poems are all mine; Rumi never gave titles to any of his poems.

Rumi's poetry of love illuminates our mind as we reflect on his words and the world we live in. As Rumi says the essential solution to all of our problems – individually, socially, and globally – is the spirit of love. Rumi addresses God as Friend or Beloved. Without friendship, and without heart-felt care and compassion, no other solution is really a solution. Only love melts greed and selfishness; only love opens our eyes to beauty and real life; and only love brings about lasting peace and real joy. Through love pain is healed.

Rasoul Shams

Salt Lake City, July 2023

LONGING

- Wanting whole-heartedly
- Striving to attain
- Insistent, restless desire
- Compelling need
- Thirst
- Yearning

1. Listen

Listen!

Listen to the reed flute and how it laments;

it relates the story of separation:

"Ever since I was cut from the reed-bed,

men and women have cried in my lament.

I seek out a heart

shredded into pieces by separation,

then only can I describe

the pain of this longing.

Whoever is left far from his origin

whoever is left far from her origin

seeks to return to the days of union."

2· Through love

Through love
bitter becomes sweet.

Through love
copper turns to gold.

Through love
dregs taste like pure wine.

Through love
pain is healed.

Through love
death begets life.

Through love
king becomes servant.

3. Fire of love

Through love
cold nature becomes warm-hearted.

In the fire of love
rigid stones soften and melt.

Do not be harsh to lovers
for not being normal.

The wine of love
has made them mad and impudent.

4. The heart is a candle

The heart is a candle
longing to be lit and illuminate.

Torn from the beloved,
the tormented heart desires
to be united.

If you do not know
what longing and burning is,
you will miss this point:
Love is not learned or taught;
love comes as grace.

5. As you walk

As you walk,
the path appears.

When you empty yourself,
you contain the universe.

When you melt,
the entire world cannot contain you.

Then you come face to face with the true You.

6. If you

If you have no beloved,
why do you not seek one?

If you have your beloved,
why do you not rejoice?

7. Someone asked

Someone asked:

"What is love?"

I said:

"Do not ask about its definition.

You will *see* love when you become like *me*.

You will start to *sing* when love calls you."

. . .

Someone asked:

"What is love?"

I said:

"You will know when *you* become *we*."

8. Seeking union

There is no lover seeking union
without a beloved searching for him as well.

A single hand's clapping cannot produce sound
without being accompanied by the other hand.

The thirsty person cries for fresh water,
while the water is groaning:
> "Who is the drinker?"

We belong to water,

      and water belongs to us.

9. Seek thirst

Do

    not

        seek

            water.

Seek

    thirst.

Then fresh water will rush forth

        from above and below.

10· You, I desire

Show me your face, darling!
To see the rose garden– I desire.

Give me a smile, sweetheart!
To taste the sweetness of life– I desire.

Show me your face, sunshine!
The dark clouds have wrapped me.
To see your warm and radiant face– I desire.

In your voice and fragrance
I hear liberating music.
I come to you always
for your bosom and arms– I desire.

Sometimes you say,

"Enough, leave me alone now."

Even when you say that,

to hear your voice– I desire.

11. Love says

Reason says:

> "These six directions –
> north, south, east, west, up, and down –
> are the limits.
> There is no way out!"

Love says:

> "Oh yes, there is a way.
> I have traveled it many times."

Reason sees a market and begins to trade.
Love sees treasure lands beyond this market.

12. The sky is in love

If the Sky were not in love
its chest would not be serene and splendid.

If the Sun were not in love
its face would not be beautiful and bright.

If the Earth were not in love
no plant could sprout out from her heart.

If the Sea were not aware of love
it would have remained motionless somewhere.

13· Branches

The tree's branches draw water
from the lowermost point to the top.

Likewise, love uplifts our souls.
No need for a ladder.

14. Enter the fire

Put aside tricks and deceit;
be sincere and love-mad.
Go and wash off all the hatred from your chest,
    seven times with water.
Like the moth enter the fire of love.
Then, you shall become our companion,
    drinking from the wine of love.

15. Friends

With friends
>   you fly with your wings.

Without friends
>   you are a single fallen feather.

Flying with your wings
>   you master the wind.

As a single feather
>   the wind blows you in all directions.

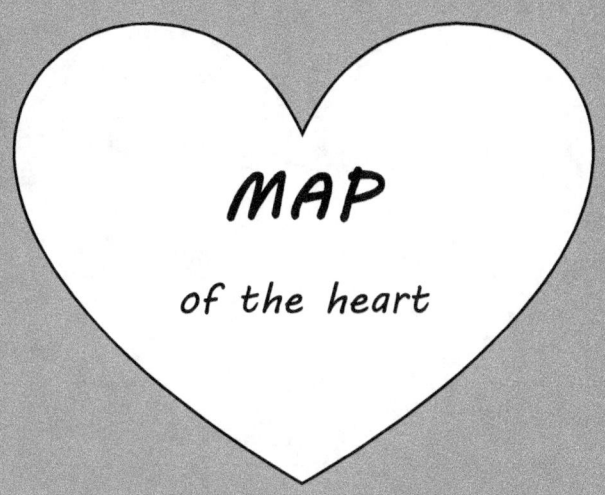

MAP
of the heart

MAP

- Representation of an area on a flat diagram
- Survey
- Plan
- Location

16. Love stays awake

The love in my heart never sleeps;
even when my eyes fall asleep,
love stays awake.

There is one more thing,
but I cannot say it
because the love in my heart
is silent about it too.

17· A stranger in this world

Why does the heart feel that
it is a stranger in the whole world?

Because the heart comes from
beyond space and time,
and "placelessness"
keeps it apart from all these places.

18. Finding a home

Whoever is not attached to this world
finds a home in the heart.

Nowhere in this universe
is more spacious than the heart.

19. Where God resides

A prophet once said that God had revealed this to him:

> *"I am not contained in any one place,*
> *above or below;*
> *on the Earth or in the Sky,*
> *not even on the Divine Throne*
> *as people imagine.*
> *Strangely, however, I am*
> *in the hearts of the faithful.*
> *If you wish to find me,*
> *seek me in those hearts."*

20. A pure mirror

Sufis are those who have polished their chests
clean from greed, desire, meanness and hatred.
The heart is, indeed, a pure mirror,
for it receives infinite images.
Sufis possess in their chests a mirror
that reflects infinite images
from the Unseen Realm.
Remember this:
The heart's mirror has no bounds.
Therefore, the intellect must remain silent
or else it will mislead you.
For the heart is with God
or indeed, God is the heart.

21. Shining heart

Do you know why the mirror of your heart
does not shine and reflect Light?

Because the rust has not been polished
from its surface.

22. Purifying water

Wash off the dust from your heart
with the purifying water of wisdom.

Then your eyes will not be bound to
this mundane world.

23. Crystal clear

My chest
>> has opened up to the Infinite.

My soul
>> filled with love, is crystal clear.

My heart
>> is a wine glass –
>>> God's wine glass.

24. A window to light

The heart is a window to Light.
The temple of the body is bright
because of the heart.
The body gradually withers;
the heart stays.
>   The heart is eternal.

25· So buoyant

The heart is so buoyant;
       it always goes upward.
The intellect, at best, can be a ladder
       to climb to the rooftop.

When my heart hears that the beloved is coming,
it overflows with love and
       rushes to the rooftop
to look for the signs of the beloved.

Looking for signs of the beloved,
a world beyond this world comes to my sight.

I could see the whole ocean in a jar,
and the heaven on earth.

26· Origin of the heart

The body – for it came from sperm,
flows down like water.

The heart – for its origin is fire,
flows heavenward.

27. Source of all songs

The source of all songs is the heart,
although the sounds are heard
in the mountain of the body.

After you are charmed by the sound,
silently go into the source.

28. Dance until dawn

I am silent, so is my heart.
But the beloved does not sleep.

So, I have become the tongue for my beloved.
I shall sing and dance until dawn.

29. Face of the heart

The heart has a face,
but not like the face of any creature.

You can see the beauties of God
reflected on the face of the heart.

.

30. Rays of light

In the bright warm rays of light
emitting from the Heart,
within you and without you,
 this world of mud and dust has become
a beautiful and joyful life.

31. Beneath the tongue

Where is the heart?

Beneath the tongue.
When the tongue is silent,
the heart *is revealed*.
When speech is gone,
the heart *reveals*.

32. Lips shut tight

When the lips are shut tight,
 the heart speaks in a hundred tongues.
This is called *mysterium*.

33. Path of the heart

The path of argumentation is
    bigotry,
        criticism, and
             justification.

The path of the heart is
    clear vision,
        joy, and
            sweet gratification.

34. Graceful ocean

The heart is a graceful ocean.
It produces one hundred pearls
from a droplet of the mind.

35. Without you

Without You,
my face would be pale.

Without You,
the ocean of my heart
would not produce any pearl.

36· Gate of Paradise

Close the gate of Hell and leave it behind.
What does that mean?
Do not stuff your life with greed.

Then open the gate of Paradise.
What does this mean?
Look into your pure and radiant heart.

37. Even if

Even if the whole world is filled with thorns,
the heart of the lover remains an orchard.

Even if the wheel of heaven stops whirling,
the world of lovers will function fine.

While all others are burdened
with sorrow and suffering,
the lover's soul is always
tender and kind, vivid and delightful.

38· Green garden

The green garden of love has no bounds.
It bears many kinds of fruit,
except sorrow and pleasure.

The garden of love is ever fresh and green.
It is beyond the vicissitudes of spring or autumn.

Being in love is beyond sorrow and pleasure.

39. Garden in the ocean

The heart is an inner garden –
with trees hidden and invisible.
It displays hundreds of scenes
on the same field, in the same soil.

The heart is like an ocean all around us –
without shores, without bounds.
Each wave in the ocean of the heart
causes hundreds of waves.

40. Chattering mouth

Close your chattering mouth,

and open the door of your heart,

because that is where

        souls

                converge and

                    converse.

41. Will they understand?

If I utter words, will they understand?

No. I won't talk. It's best to be silent;
otherwise, the heart will say:
>"You can't keep secrets."

UNION

- Joining together
- A unified condition
- Belonging to one entity
- Oneness

42. Created in pairs

It is Divine wisdom
        set in decree and destiny
that we have been made
        lovers of one another.
All parts and particles of this universe
        have been created in pairs,
and each one falls in love with a mate.

43. Red wine

When I drink the ruby-red wine

from my beloved's hand,

I glow like a pure gem.

My cup complains because I have drunk

so much that the wine has become me:

I have become my beloved's wine.

44. They say

They say love combined with logic is best.
They say abstinence in everything is good.

Yes, what they say may be good as gold,
but my soul devoted to the beloved
                            rejoices most.

45. Like the wave

I am a single soul,

but with a hundred thousand bodies.

It's all me. I am not talking about others.

Like the wave in the ocean, I raise my head.

Look at me closely!

My head is the same as my body.

Like the wave!

46. A hundred days

Even if you compress a hundred days
of separation into a single day,
it will not cheer up my wailing heart.

Even if we are united for a hundred days,
my heart will not be pleased with
a single day of separation.

Never mind if strangers laugh at my words:
Those who are not love-mad think too much.

47. Fusion

See how love is fused with the lovers.
See how life is fused with the soil.

Don't be a judge of this or that, good or bad.
See how, in the end, they both disappear
into none – into one.

Don't speak of this life and the after-life.
See how both worlds have merged
in this moment.

The heart is a lion king or a lovely queen;
the tongue is their messenger.
See how the heart and the tongue speak as one.

Union is our birthright; let's be together
as the earth and the sky live together.

Look at water, fire, soil, and air:
They seem to be opposites, but they blend in love.

48. Soul of the world

You are my soul, my world;
I have nothing to do with this soul or this world.

You are my ever-flowing treasure;
I have nothing to do with losses or profits.

Now I am drunk by your love;
now I am burned by the fire of this love.

Since I am circling around you,
I have nothing to do with the passage of time.

Being with you I am fulfilled and joyful;
I have no interest in other affairs.

Since I have you in my life,
my search has come to a beautiful end.

Since I am swimming in the river of your love,
I need not search for water elsewhere.

What else can I say? How can I describe
this ever-flowing river of grace that you are?

Being with you,
each particle in me becomes a universe;
each droplet of my water dances in vapor.

Since I know your name,
I have no interest in other names.

To find a pearl one has to dive into
depths of the sea.
I have dived with my whole body
into the ocean of your love;
I need not run arduously on dry land.

49. Fragrance of love

Lovers gamble away the whole world
in one breath of love.

They give away a hundred years
for a moment of union.

They travel a thousand towns
for the fragrance of each other.

Lovers devote their lives,
even a thousand lives if they have, they devote
for the sake of each other's heart.

50. Be with me

My beloved said:

"I am beauty. Be beauty.

Do you want beauty? Be with me.

Don't be a droplet of water. Be an ocean.

Do you want an ocean? Be with me."

51. Inside the eye

In every star, I see a charming eye.
In every eye, I see a shining star –
an angel inside the eye.
Cross-eyes see one object as two.
My two eyes see two as one.

52· Only one light

The lamps, whatever they are made of,
are numerous; but their Light is the same.
The Light comes from beyond.

If your sight is fixated on the lamps,
you will be confused because of
their multitude and multiple forms.

But if you gaze upon the Light,
you will be freed from the confusion of
this *versus* that in the crowd of
forms and numbers.

If you want to see the kernel of life,
remember this:
> Conflicts among religions arise
> from fixation on their perspectives.

53. How I became human

I died to the mineral and became plant.

I died to the plant and became animal.

I died to the animal and became human.

So why fear?
When have I been diminished by dying?

Likewise, I should die to this being human
and fly with the angel's wings.

And I should cross even the angelic river;
For all things perish save the Divine face.

Once more, I shall die as an angel,
and become that which cannot even be imagined.

I shall become utterly empty, no-thing.
From that empty space,
I hear an organ, singing to me:
Verily, unto That shall we all return.

54. You and I

Happy is the hour when we sit together
in a balcony facing a green garden – you and I.
Two bodies in one passionate soul – you and I.

Happy is the hour when we walk into the garden,
hand in hand – you and I.
And the colorful garden and the singing birds
confer upon us the Water of Life.

When the night comes,
the stars of the sky visit us.
And we display to them
our beautiful love – you and I.

You and I, with no "You" and no "I," united in joy,
and free from the scattered, disturbing thoughts.
Joyful and free – you and I.

AGONY

- "Contest for victory" (Greek)
- Intense mental or physical pain
- Severe suffering; anguish
- Distress before death
- Outburst of emotions

55. Ups and downs

In love,

        there is union with the beloved,

and separation   from the beloved.

The path has ups

                and

                        downs.

56· I asked love

One night I asked Love:

> Tell me truly, what are you?

Love said:

> I am life eternal, I bestow joy upon joy.

I asked:

> Oh you, who are outside of space and time,
>
> where is your real home?

Love said:

> I am a companion to the heart's fire;
>
> I sit beside wet eyes.

57. Love-madness

Love-madness is different from all other illnesses.
Love is the celestial guide to the Divine mysteries.
A lover may be drawn this way or that way.
But, in the end, all devoted lovers
enter the Palace of Love.

58. Inside the ruined heart

God's treasure is hidden in the ruined heart.
Much treasure is found in the ruins.

...

Where there is a ruined place,
there is hope for treasure.
Seek God's treasure in your broken heart.

59. Dark shadow

Your ego casts a dark shadow on your life.
Let it melt in the rays of the Sun.
How long will you follow and look at the shadow?
Look instead at the Light.

60. Healing medicine

Oh, my heart!
Sit with a person who understands the heart.
Sit under a tree which has fresh flowers.
In the market of drug sellers
do not wander hither and thither aimlessly.
Go to the shop which has the healing medicine.
Not every eye has eyesight.
Not every sea contains jewels.

61. Sorrows of the world

Even if sorrow engulfs the whole world,
it will not touch the one consumed in love.
A particle dancing in love
conquers the whole world by being the world.

62. The real step

They say one has to go through love
                  step   by   step.
That may be true, but the real step
is taken by your eternal legs.

In the house of your mind you see
a multitude of things,
but that house is full of fantasy.

Rub your eyes and look again:
                Emptiness   is   Eternal.

63. Fear not

For everyone thirsty of love
> there is a special wine.

Fear not!

If your jar runs out of water,
> there is still abundant water for you.

Fear not!

Even if they ruin this house, remember this:
> Treasures are found within the ruins.

Fear not!

Wake up from the sleep of this world.

Fear not!

64. Agony of love

An impatient lover is most helpless
because her illness cannot be easily cured.
The agony of love cannot be healed
by being possessive and selfish.
True love does not brag about loyalty,
nor does it fancy disloyalty.
Love transcends loyalty and disloyalty.

65· Now run

I shouted. Love said, "Be silent."

I became quiet. Love said, "Say something."

I moved around. Love said, "Be still."

I stopped. Love said, "Now run."

66. I am ripe

Oh, my heart!
Who has ever seen morning light
in the midst of night?
Who has ever seen a sincere lover
to be a famed, distinguished person?
You cry and say: I am burned in love.
Do not cry out.
Who has ever heard a ripe fruit cry,
"I am ripe"?

67· I have chosen you

In this entire world I have chosen you.
Is it fair that I sit here sad and hurt
because of this love?

My heart is like a pen in your hand.
Whether I am happy or sad it is your writing.

I desire none other than what you desire.
Beauty to my eye is what you display.

You bring out the best in me –
        now a rose, now a thorn.
That is why sometime I smell roses and
        other times I touch thorns.

I am howsoever you treat me.
I am whatsoever you think of me.

68· Love is a mystery

Love is not a matter of pretention.
The path of love is a mystery;
it is paved with profound meanings of life.

Law cannot answer the lover's quest.
Law is about property; loving is not possessing.
The mystery of love runs deep into no-thingness.

ECSTASY

- Standing outside oneself" (Greek)
- An intense feeling of joy
- Frenzy; passion
- Bliss; paradise
- Elation; rapture
- Mystical trance

69. This love

O God, this love,
> how hidden it is;
> how visible it is.

It is like intoxicating wine;

It is like the luminous Moon.

O God, this love has decorated
> our soul and the universe.

70. Delight

No love, no delight.
Without love, life has no balance.
Millions of raindrops may pour
from the clouds upon the earth,
but only in their ecstasy of love,
will they selflessly create a green garden.

71. Never, never

O my love, will I ever be tired of you?
Never. Never.

Will I ever take another beloved?
Never. Never.

In the garden of our union
I am immersed in flowers.
Away from you I face a thorny life.
Will I ever want this?
Never. Never.

72. I will win life

If I lose my heart for your love,
>I will win life.

Whatever I offer you,
>you return a thousand times more.

When your lovely hair graces my hands,
>I win any game in any field of the world.

73. I became alive

I was dead; I became alive.
I was all cries; I became laughter.
The glory of love came upon me,
and I became everlasting glory.
Now my eyes are satisfied and content,
 and my soul has the courage of a lion.
And I am the shining Venus in the sky of life.

74. All particles are lovers

Not a single straw can move save by a wind,
how can then this universe move
without the wind of passion and longing?

All parts and particles of the universe are lovers,
 and every lover is intoxicated
by the sight and beauty of the beloved.

75. Only one step

If you are not drunk,
you lag behind all pilgrims.
When you are selfless,
there is only one step between
you and your Mecca.

76. Die in this love

Die! Die! Die in this love.
When your small self dies in this love,
you attain the vast spirit.
Die! And don't fear this death!
When you sprout out from this soil,
you reach to the high heaven.
Die! Die and be free from your mind.
For the mind is a prison and you are a captive.
Take an axe and dig a hole though the prison.
When you come out of the prison,
you are the master.
Die! Die before the beloved's face.
For when your "I" dies before the beloved
you become the lion king.
Die! Die and go beyond the dark cloud.
For behind the cloud you are the shining sun.

77. As long as I live

As long as I live, love is my life –
my peace, my rest, my support and my solace;
my every day work and my destiny in the world.

Loving, lover and beloved are wrapped in one.

78. Most wondrous

Love is most wondrous!

All beings belong to love.

Love joins the hearts and also breaks them.

Love is always home; lovers are her doorkeepers.

Love is our mother; we are the children of love.

79. Wind and leaf

You are the wind; I am the leaf.

How can I not dance?

You give me real work to do.

What else would I do?

With a small heavenly stone

you hit the jar I carry around.

My broken jar pours out pearls and jewels.

This is how it is between you and me.

80. Shining like the sun

The beloved shines like the sun,

and the lover circles her like a planet.

Love is the particle that makes up sunlight.

When the spring wind blows

all trees dance except the dead ones.

81. Consider this

Consider this:
The whirling heavens and the wheel of life
are all turned by the waves of love.
Without love, the world would freeze and decay.
Without love, how can minerals disappear
To become plants?
Without love, how can plants die
To become the human soul?
Without love, how can the soul be the Holy Spirit
whose breath made Mary pregnant?

82. Love is this

Love is this:
To fly heavenward, and
with each breath tear a veil of ignorance.

At the first breath, go beyond yourself.
At the last step, walk without feet.

Love is this:
Not to set your eye on the mundane world,
 but to see beyond your eye.

I said to my heart:
Congratulations!
You are now in the circle of lovers.
You can see what lies behind.
You can walk in paradise.

LIVING

- Being alive
- Not dead
- Energetic and mobile
- Vivid
- Dwelling

83. Plant seeds of love

In this earth

In this soil

In this pure field

Let's not plant any seed

Other than seeds of compassion and love.

84. Source of all joy

Being with you is the source of all joy.
You are the real meaning of all things that I see.
Do not break from me even for a moment,
for a boat cannot sail without water.
I am a book containing many errors;
as you read the book I am corrected.

85. Water of life

Being with you means drinking
From the Water of Life.
You only know my way to liberation.
Do not leave my sight
for you are the light of my eye.
Do not leave my heart
for you are the delight of my soul.
When I do not see you
my soul cries; my heart weeps.

Oh no! Who am I to claim you for my life?
Who am I to call you to my side?
It is *your grace* that draws me to you.

86. History of lovers

Love comes from beginningless time.
Love will remain for eternity.
Countless are the seekers of love.
On the Day of Reckoning
those who were not lovers have been losers.

87. Days of life

Do not count
    those days of your life
        as really lived
            if you were not a lover.

88. Love is for the living

Life must be lived in love.

The dead are not supposed to do that.

Do you know who is alive?

The one who is refreshed every moment by love.

89. The unseen

In the realm of the Unseen,
there is sandal wood burning.
This love is the smoke of that incense.

From a colorless, formless Being
has come all these colorful forms.

90. The book

The book of the Sufi

is not filled with bookish knowledge or words.

The book of the Sufi

is none other than the heart – white as snow.

91. Empty bowl

Empty bowl
> you dance on water.

Overfilled
> you drown.

92. Stay by her side

I won't leave this bright house for darkness.
I won't leave this blessed place for anywhere else.
Here I am with my beloved and our love
      and the rest of our lives.
I won't leave her side
even if the world drags me away.

Even if the world is flooded with ocean waves,
I won't be swayed;
I will stay with my precious pearl.
I have found the kernel;
I won't settle with the shell.
I live in safety; I won't invite disaster.

93. Diamond-sharp sword

Do not take a wooden sword into battle.
Always review your work first
    so that it does not end up in failure.
If your sword is wooden,
    get instead a diamond-sharp sword.
Then move forward with joy.

The diamond-sharp sword for
the spiritual warrior is made
in the workshop of God's Friends.
Indeed, to meet such a master of the heart
is a rare transforming experience.
All wise wayfarers have said this:
A great wise mystic is God's mercy to all people.

94. Who am I?

What can you call me, o people?
For I do not identify myself with what you think.

Neither Christian, nor Jew,
nor Pagan, nor Moslem.

I am not Eastern or Western,
Neither from lands nor from the seas.
I am not of minerals nor of the circling planets.

I am not of soil or water. I am not of air or fire.
I am not of the sky or of earth.
I am not of this cosmos.

I am not of this world, nor of the next.
I am not from Paradise or from Hell.
I am not of Adam or Eve.
I did not fall from the Garden of Eden.

Placeless. No address.
No body. No soul.
I simply belong to the Soul of All.

I have put away duality;
I see the two worlds as one.
> I seek One;
>> I know One;
>>> I see One;
>>>> I sing One.

95. A divine person

A divine person is drunken without wine.

A divine person is full without meat.

A divine person is full of wonder.

A divine person is not asleep.

A divine person is royal in simple clothes.

A divine person is a treasure hidden in a ruin.

A divine person is not of this air and earth.

A divine person is not of fire and water either.

A divine person is boundless.

A divine person rains pearls without a cloud.

A divine person contains bright moons and suns.

A divine person has wisdom from the source.

A divine person is not attached to hearsay.

A divine person does not identify with

    dogmas and opinions –

    religious or otherwise.

A divine person is not obsessed with
        this "right" and that "wrong."
A divine person is the rider of a glorious horse,
who has ridden here from the unseen world.
A divine person is concealed in
the sunshine of faith.
To find your divine person, be a seeker.

96. Our sweet words

Those sweet words
we have said to each other
are concealed in the heart of the sky.

One day, those words
will become raindrops and
the secret of our love
will sprout from the soil.

97. Fear of death

Everyone fears death; Sufis laugh at it.

Nothing of this world terrifies their hearts;
because they know that a strike on
the oyster shell does not destroy the pearl inside.

They know this not from words and scriptures.

Their knowledge comes from
their being empty and poor in spirit.

98. Religion of love

The religion of love is separate from religions.
It is not limited to any form of religion.
Lovers belong to God.
Beloved is their religion.

99. Neither captive nor captor

Other than being a captive or a captor,
there is a third state.
When I am in that state of peace and emptiness,
I lament for both the captive and the captor.
What is the state of peace and emptiness?
It is like dreamless sleep at night:
The captor is not a captor;
the captive is not a captive.

100· Arrived

I have arrived in a meadow
>wherein love grows.
Whatever dirt is brought here
>becomes all clean and pure.

101. Outcome of my life

The outcome of my life

is no more than these three lines:

> I was a raw material;
>
> I was cooked and matured;
>
> I was baked and burned.

*Through Love
Pain Is Healed*

SOURCES

Rumi's poetry is contained in two great books: The *Divân-e Shams* and the *Masnavi*, both in Persian. In selecting and translating this anthology I have used the following editions of these two books.

D [*Divan*] containing Sonnets or Odes (O) and Quatrains (Q)

Mowlânâ Jalâluddin Mohammad Balkhi Rumi, *Kulliât-e Shams-e Tabrizi* (*Divân-e Shams or Divân-e Kabir*), ten volumes, edited by Badi uz-Zamân Foruzânfar (Tehran University Press, 1957-1967; republished by Amir Kabir Press, Tehran, 1976). The *Divân* ("Poetry Collection") contains Rumi's 3500 lyrical odes (O) and 1900 quatrains (Q). A few odes (O) "attributed" to Rumi come from Reynold Nicholson's anthology (N): *Selected Poems from the Divani Shamsi Tabrizi* (Cambridge University Press, 1898).

M [*Masnavi*, pronounced *Mathnawi* in Arabic]

Mowlânâ Jalâluddin Mohammad Balkhi Rumi, *Masnavi-e Ma'navi* ("Spiritual Couplets"), edited by Reynold Nicholson (*The Mathnawi of Jalaluddin Rumi*, eight volumes, 1925-1940, Cambridge University Press for the E.J.W. Gibb Memorial; single Persian volume printed by Amir Kabir Press, Tehran, 1957, reprinted numerous times). This book contains Rumi's parables and teachings in about 26,000 verses arranged in six volumes.

Sources for the poems in the present anthology are given after their numbers on the following pages.

1) M, I: 1-4
2) M, II: 1529-31
3) D-Q 795
4) D-Q 1881
5) D-Q 742
6) D-O 3061: 32589
7) D-O: 29050-51;
   M, II: Prologue
8) M, III: 4393-97
9) M, III: 3212
10) D-O 441
11) D-O 132: 1522-23
12) D-O 2674: 28369-72
13) D-O 1940: 20472
14) D-O 2131: 22547-49
15) D-Q 1872
16) D-Q 952
17) D-O 2725 28934
18) D-O 425: 4477
19) M, I, 2652-54
20) M, I, 3484-3489
21) M, I: 34
22) D-O 771: 8049
23) D-O 185: 2047
24) D-O 898: 9411
25) D-O 2730: 29013-16
26) D-O 1125: 11879
27) M, V: 24165
28) D-O 83: 973
29) D-O 1001: 10570
30) D-O 706: 7386
31) D-O 803: 8408
32) D-O 873: 9139
33) D-O 1148: 12187
34) D-O 628: 6556
35) D-O 138: 1581
36) D-O: 34717
37) D-O 662: 6914-16
38) M, I: 1802-03
39) D-Q 1429
40) D-O 110: 1248
41) D-O 455: 4822
42) M, III: 4400-01
43) D-Q 50
44) D-Q 245
45) D-Q 1237
46) D-Q 1729
47) D-O 2381
48) D-O 162
49) D-Q 688
50) D-Q 1464
51) D-Q 1263
52) M, III: 1255-58
53) M, III: 3901-07
54) D-O 2214

55) D-O 2742: 29156
56) D-O 1402: 14851-52
57) M, I: 110-111
58) D-O: 3104: 33114; 141: 1613
59) D-O 1938: 20395
60) D-O 563: 5960-61
61) D-Q 410
62) D-Q 263
63) D-Q 986
64) D-Q 134
65) D-Q 1281
66) D-Q 844
67) D-O 1521
68) D-Q 391
69) D-O 95: 1059-61
70) D-Q 805
71) D-Q 1915
72) D-Q 1187
73) D-O 1393: 14741-14742
74) D-O 2674: 28365-65
75) D-O 865: 9060
76) D-O 636
77) D-Q 310
78) D-Q 828
79) D-Q 1900
80) D-Q 466
81) M, V: 3854-56
82) D-O 1919
83) D-O 1475: 15558
84) D-O 2756: 29290-92
85) D-O 2733: 29042-45
86) D-Q 754
87) D-O 974: 10315
88) D-O 843: 8824
89) D-O 2949: 31322
90) M, II: 159
91) D-O 3057: 32544
92) D-O 1653: 17320-22 & 17330
93) M, I: 714-717
94) N-O 31 "attributed"
95) N-O 8 "attributed"
96) D-Q 1283
97) M, I: 3495-97
98) M, II: 1770
99) D-O 1746: 18309-10
100) D-O 583: 6174
101) "Attributed," possibly derived from D: 18521

Acknowledgments

All translators of Rumi owe a great debt of gratitude to two eminent scholars who produced critical editions of Rumi's poetry works based on the numerous ancient manuscripts extant in various libraries in Asia and Europe: Professor Reynold Nicholson (1868-1945) of Cambridge University who edited a scholarly edition of the *Masnavi* based on various manuscripts and Professor Badi-uz Zaman Foruzânfar (1900-1970) of Tehran University who accomplished the same daunting task for the *Divân*. They devoted several decades of their lives to these works. Rumi's works have been a four-decade exploration for me, and I am delighted to be a student of this great spiritual poet and master of the path of love. The draft of the current translation was kindly read by four dear friends: Florin Nielsen, Teresa May Habibian, Marie English, and Margo Andrews. I am very grateful for their helpful edits and suggestions; nevertheless, I alone am responsible for any possible error in the final version.

About this Book

Translated from the Persian, this book is a collection of 101 short poems and inspirational teachings by Rumi about love and the life of the heart.

The Translator

Rasoul Shams is the founder of the Rumi Poetry Club. His previous books include *Rumi: The Art of Loving* (2012), *Rumi Essays* (2016), and *The Words of Rumi* (2017).

The Publisher

The Rumi Poetry Club was founded in 2007 on the occasion of the 800th anniversary of Rumi's birth in order to foster spiritual literature and art. RUMI PUBLICATIONS is an imprint of the Rumi Poetry Club. For more information visit:

www.rumipoetryclub.com

About the Poet

Jalâluddin Rumi (30 September 1207 to 17 December 1273) was an eminent Persian Sufi poet and mystic who composed nearly 70,000 verses of poetry centered on love.

About the Cover Painting

The miniature painting ("The Lovers") on the cover page of the book is by the renowned Persian painter Reza Abbasi in about 1630 during the Safavid dynasty in Iran. Using watercolor, ink and gold on paper, the painting was made in Isfahan, the Safavid capital. The miniature depicts two lovers embracing each other. The original work is currently in the Metropolitan Museum of Art in New York City. It was purchased and gifted to the museum by Francis Weld in 1950. The image is in public domain on the website of the Metropolitan Museum of Art.

Notes

Notes

Notes

Notes

www.ingramcontent.com/pod-product-compliance
Lightning Source LLC
Chambersburg PA
CBHW052308300426
44110CB00035B/2178